Grief and
Your Child

....

Sharing God's Comfort in Loss

Bob Kellemen

newgrowthpress.com

New Growth Press, Greensboro, NC 27404
newgrowthpress.com

Scripture quotations are from THE HOLY BIBLE, NEW INTERNATIONAL VERSION®, NIV® Copyright © 1973, 1978, 1984, 2011 by Biblica, Inc.® Used by permission. All rights reserved worldwide.

Names and identifying details in counseling vignettes have been changed to protect the privacy and confidentiality of individuals and families.

Cover Design: Trish Mahoney, themahoneystudio.com
Interior Design and Typesetting: Gretchen Logterman

ISBN: 978-1-64507-178-5 (Print)
ISBN: 978-1-64507-179-2 (eBook)

Library of Congress Cataloging-in-Publication Data
Names: Kellemen, Robert W., author.
Title: Grief and your child : sharing God's comfort in loss / by Bob Kellemen.
Description: Greensboro, NC : New Growth Press, [2021] | Includes bibliographical references. | Summary: "Counselor and author Bob Kellemen walks parents through the stages of grief so they can better understand the challenges their child is facing and help them navigate the long and difficult road of lament and recovery"-- Provided by publisher.
Identifiers: LCCN 2021007481 (print) | LCCN 2021007482 (ebook) | ISBN 9781645071785 (print) | ISBN 9781645071792 (ebook)
Subjects: LCSH: Grief in children--Religious aspects--Christianity. | Parent and child--Religious aspects--Christianity.
Classification: LCC BV4906 .K45 2021 (print) | LCC BV4906 (ebook) | DDC 248.8/45--dc23
LC record available at https://lccn.loc.gov/2021007481
LC ebook record available at https://lccn.loc.gov/2021007482

Printed in India
28 27 26 25 24 23 22 21   1 2 3 4 5

The Greatest Grief

Nothing shakes your child's life like the death of a loved one. Your child's entire world feels shattered, and nothing seems okay in the aftermath of such devastating loss.

Maybe the lost loved one is a beloved elementary school teacher who is there one day and gone the next—tragically killed by a drunk driver in a car accident. Perhaps the loved one is a childhood best friend who has endured chemo for months and now has succumbed to cancer. Or that lost loved one is someone you, as your child's parent, also love deeply—your spouse, your parent, one of your other children—and you too are grieving deeply.

Ministering to Your Child's Grieving Heart

My goal is to help you to better understand and empathize with your child's grieving heart so that you can minister God's comfort to your son or daughter. To move toward this goal, you'll journey with me as I introduce you to Jared and his family. You'll sit in and observe as I counsel Jared through the loss of his grandfather, so you can identify with your own child's grief journey.

Even though I'm a biblical counselor and an equipper of counselors, I've often said that *children need loving and wise parents more than they need loving and wise counselors*. That's why our counseling vignette with Jared and his family is not meant so much to equip counselors but to equip parents—to equip *you.* No human being can comfort a grieving child quite like that child's parent. And no one can comfort a grieving child like the One who is a Man of Sorrows, acquainted with grief (Isaiah 53:3). My desire is to help you usher your child into Christ's comforting embrace.

Jared's Journey

As ten-year-old Jared was walking home with a friend from a local park, he was surprised to see his mom drive up.

"Get in the car, Jared. Your grandfather just passed away."

Shocked by these abrupt words, Jared responded blankly, "You're kidding"—as if his mom would tease about something like this. But that's what shock will do.

The next few days were a whirlwind. Grandpa's death was unexpected. This was Jared's first experience with the death of anyone close to him, and he was totally unprepared. So was his family.

They attended our church once or twice a year, on holidays, but at this point Jared's parents had not made a personal commitment to Christ. The funeral visitation was at an Eastern Orthodox Church where Jared's grandparents had been nominally involved. No one prepared Jared for what he would experience. Walking into the visitation in his stiff new suit and tie, Jared was immediately hit with an unfamiliar odor—incense used by the Orthodox priest.

Jared was then ushered forward to the open casket. He was terrified. He'd never seen a dead body, except on TV. Grandpa was so pale. So stiff. So . . . dead.

Jared's whole body reacted—he felt sick to his stomach, his palms were sweaty, his heart raced, and he thought he was going to faint. He wanted to be anywhere but there.

Then the first of several visitation services began. The Orthodox priest entered, waving an incense holder and singing . . . or was it chanting . . . in *another* language. It was all so otherworldly for Jared—creepy, scary, and petrifying.

The funeral and burial were difficult enough, but then a more traumatic incident occurred. A week after the funeral, Jared's mom, in an almost offhanded comment, said, "Last night I was in the kitchen and I thought I heard Grandpa call out my name. It was so weird. . . . "

Now paralyzing fear had been added to Jared's grief and confusion. *Would Grandpa haunt me, too?* he worried. That night Jared lay in bed, stiff as a board, afraid to close his eyes in the dark, wondering whether his Grandpa would appear to him.

Thus began several weeks of barely sleeping. Jared needed not just a night light but the full room light on. He needed someone in his room until, out of exhaustion, he final dozed off.

Mom and Dad felt clueless to help. They first went to their family doctor, who recommended counseling and prescribed a mild sleeping pill "to take the edge off." Then Jared's parents remembered hearing about free counseling at our church and decided, "Let's call and see if they can help Jared."

Mom and Dad (Elyse and Dexter) called the church and explained their need. "Our son is not handling the death of his grandfather well at all. He can't sleep. He's terrified Grandpa is going to appear to him. We're at our wits' end."

Our counseling department receptionist shared that I, as counseling pastor, worked with a lot of families dealing with grief. She explained that with a child's Jared's age, I typically preferred to meet first with the parents so I could understand the issues clearly; I also liked to keep the parents involved throughout the counseling. She confirmed that Elyse and Dexter would be okay with this arrangement.

"As long as he can meet with us *soon*, it'll be fine!"

The next day I had my initial appointment with Elyse and Dexter. They shared more of their concerns, the history of what had happened, how they had responded, how Jared was doing, and how they were doing. We also discussed what "successful" counseling would look like in their eyes—what end goal they were hoping for.

The Bible as Our Lens for Grief Counseling

I added one more piece to our conversation. Since they rarely attended church, I wanted to be sure they understood the basis for my counseling. "Dexter and Elyse, I can tell that you care about

Jared and are very concerned for him. Your entire family is going through a difficult, but very normal, time of grieving. I'd be delighted to offer my help." I could barely finish those words before they were thanking me effusively.

Then I continued, "You guys laughed a little sheepishly when you said, 'We don't come here very often.' Since you may not know exactly how we do things around here, I want to be sure we're all on the same page about what to expect. You can tell from our first hour together that I'm not going to 'beat you over the head with the Bible.' However (I held my Bible at my eye level), I will seek to have all of my counsel come from a biblical worldview. The Bible will be my lens for helping Jared—and you—think through how to handle death and grief. There is no way to find hope as we face death and no way to find healing as we deal with grief other than through God's Word and God's Son." Having agreed to this focus, we made plans for Dexter and Elyse to bring Jared in to see me the next day.

The Grief Journey

In understanding children's struggles with death and grief, I use a modified version of a grief journey model I outlined in my book *God's Healing for Life's Losses*.[1] In it, I seek to help children and their parents move from the typical *natural* response to death, to a biblical *supernatural* response to death by facing loss face-to-face with Christ.

The Grief Journey:
Facing Loss Face-to-Face with Christ[2]

Typical Human Grief Response	Biblical Redeemed Grief Response
Denial/Isolation	Candor: Honesty with Yourself
Anger/Resentment	Complaint/Lament: Honesty with God
Bargaining/Works	Crying Out to God: Asking God for Help
Depression/Alienation	Comfort: Receiving God's Help

Journey Marker #1: Moving (Slowly) from Pretending to Honesty

When Jared's parents told him they were taking him to a counselor, he was upset.

"Who is he? Why am I going?" When they told Jared my name, his eyes lit up. "I know him! He's the pastor dude who's also a wrestling coach. He coached me at camp last summer. I like him!"

During our first joint meeting, we collaboratively decided how we would organize our meetings each week. Jared, Dexter, Elyse, and I would all meet together for the first fifteen minutes and the final fifteen minutes; Jared and I would meet together for the middle thirty minutes.

During the middle of our first meeting, after hearing how Jared's wrestling season was going, we shifted focus. "I understand from Mom and Dad that the whole family is having a hard time with the loss of your grandfather. I think you called him 'Grandpa,' right?"

After Jared shared a bit, I sensed that he felt embarrassed that he—a wrestler—was so fearful. So I shared some of my past struggles with fears related to death. "Even tough-guy wrestlers like us can be afraid. Death is a big opponent."

I then explained to Jared that one of the ways people try to deal with death, loss, and fear is to pretend—to deny that it happened. I mentioned casually that his response to his mom when she told him about Grandpa's death—"You're kidding"—is a common form of denial or pretending. To help Jared picture the problem with denial, I asked if he ever tried to keep a beach ball below the water when his family was on their annual Florida beach vacation. He laughed. "Oh yeah! It always squirms around and pops waaay up into the air!"

"Denial or pretending is like that, Jared. We try not to face the pain of losing Grandpa, but it comes up somewhere. I wonder if part of where it's coming up is in your fears at night. Did you know that the Bible talks about moving from pretending to being honest?" We then read Psalm 42:5 together: "Why, my soul, are you downcast? Why so disturbed within me?"

"David was a tough guy. A king. A warrior. Yet he felt sad and anxious, depressed and fearful. But instead of pretending, he was honest with himself. Instead of letting his emotions talk to him, *David talked back to his emotions.* Do you think you and I could do that? I'll go first if you want. I'll share some of the fears and sadness I've had when I've lost loved ones. Then you can go next."

So, we shared stories—fear stories and sadness stories. What started in this first meeting continued for a couple meetings, including in-between meetings as I asked Jared to write down additional fear and sadness stories and show them to me and his parents each week.

Before Jared's parents returned for our final fifteen minutes, Jared and I discussed how much he wanted Mom and Dad to know. In Jared's case, he wanted me to help him share everything with them. So, week by week, Dexter and Elyse began to gain a glimpse into their son's grieving heart and to learn the approaches we were using to help process this difficult loss.

Journeying (Patiently) with Your Child from Pretending to Honesty

As you prayerfully ponder your child's grief journey, do you detect any denial? In what ways might your son or daughter be pretending, pushing down awareness, or refusing to think about the loss?

Sometimes, as was true for Jared, one way to help a child slowly face loss is for an adult—you, as a parent—to share your story of facing loss. What has loss been like for you? Were there any ways in which you tried to pretend that the loss didn't happen? What feelings have accompanied your grief experiences?

If you were sitting in on your son or daughter's grief counseling session, what fear stories and sadness stories do you think you might be hearing? How could you begin to listen long and patiently to your son or daughter, to glance into their grieving heart, and journey with them as they slowly move back and forth between denial and honesty?

Journey Marker #2: Moving from Anger to Venting and Lamenting to God—Our Big and Loving Shepherd-King

As Jared, his parents, and I continued on this grief journey, I mentioned that for a lot of people, once they quit pretending, they end up admitting how angry they are—angry that their loved one died and that God allowed this to happen. I said, "A lot of people end up shaking their fists at God, seeing him like an unfair wrestling referee."

During one of our meetings when his parents were outside, Jared reminded me that he had attended Vacation Bible School at our church. "When I was just a kid—nine—I asked Jesus to be my Savior. But I don't think Mom and Dad have done that yet." We talked further about this, and I sensed that Jared truly knew Jesus.

"So, Jared, could we talk again about Warrior-King David and how he talked to God? David not only talked to his own soul—like we saw in Psalm 42:5—but David also talked *to God*. When he was upset, he vented and lamented. That means he told God whatever was in his heart. He knew that God knew everything he was thinking anyway. David knew that God was big enough to handle whatever he felt, so he shared his heart with God. People can do that when they have a biblical picture of God as both *big* and *loving*. Could we look at a biblical picture of God from Isaiah 40:10–11?" We read the passage together.

> See, the Sovereign LORD comes with power, and he rules with a mighty arm. See, his reward is with him, and his recompense accompanies him. He tends his flock like a shepherd: He gathers the lambs in his arms and carries them close to his heart; he gently leads those that have young.

We talked about how verse 10 pictures God as a big/strong king and how verse 11 pictures God as a loving/caring shepherd. Understanding that God is both *big* and *loving* opened Jared up to venting and lamenting—sharing his fears, sadness, and anger with God.

Together we read Psalm 13 and Psalm 88 as two examples of God's people doing just that. Over several meetings and in between meetings, Jared was able to give voice to his emotions—this time not just to himself, but also to his *big* and *loving* Savior—to his Shepherd-King.

Journeying (Together) with Your Child from Anger to Venting and Lamenting to God

As you think about your child's grief response, have you detected any anger? Sometimes it seeps out in odd and unexpected ways—anger over loss ends up in an eruption over a sibling taking away a toy or standing in front of the TV. Other times grief-anger explodes at you with the least provocation.

What is it like for *you* to talk to God honestly about your feelings—to vent and lament like David did? As a family, how could you practice the biblical art of psalm-like lamenting to God?

When your child is ready, what would it look like for you to read a psalm of lament together, and for each of you to say or write your lament to God? How could you introduce your child to the God of Isaiah 40:10–11, to their big and loving Shepherd-King?

Journey Marker #3: Moving from Self-Dependence to Crying Out to God—Who Hears and Cares, Delivers and Saves

As the weeks went by, Elyse and Dexter reported that good things were happening with Jared. He seemed more at peace. Less fearful. But his night terrors and sleep anxieties were still a struggle.

As Jared and I continued on our trek together, I explained another typical stage as people try to handle their grief when a loved one dies. "They try to manipulate or con God." Jared thought that was ridiculous.

"God's too strong to be man . . . manip . . . how do you say it? And he's too smart to be conned!"

I gave the example of a father who might try to strike a bargain with God, "I'll quit drinking if you'll cure my daughter of leukemia." I mentioned that we sometimes try to use God like Aladdin's genie in a bottle.

Then we discussed what to do instead. "We cry out to God in humble dependence. While God won't be manipulated, he does love to rescue us when we humbly cry out to him."

Jared and his parents had recently seen the school play *Oliver*, where young Oliver meekly and respectfully asks the master of the orphanage, "Please, sir, can I have some more food?" I mentioned, "That should be our posture toward our Shepherd-King: arms held up with an empty bowl, pleading for more, asking humbly for help." We then read together Psalm 34:17–18: "The righteous cry out, and the LORD hears them; he delivers them from all their troubles. The LORD is close to the broken-hearted and saves those who are crushed in spirit." I reminded Jared that God is not like the master in the orphanage who erupted in anger at Oliver's request. Instead, he loves to hear his children's cries for help.

After talking through what Jared was afraid of at night—what he thought would happen if Grandpa appeared to him—we then brought biblical truth to bear on those fears, including biblical images of God. When his night terrors struck, Jared began to cry out in prayer to the Lord who was not only his Shepherd-King, but also, to use Jared's hyphenated phrase, "God-Who-Hears-and-Cares-Delivers-and-Saves!"

Journeying with Your Child from Self-Dependence to Crying Out to God

So much of good parenting starts with godly modeling. Be honest—for your sake and your child's

sake. Take your "spiritual dependence temperature."
As you face life's losses, do you try to depend upon
your own strength, or do you cry out in humility to
God? What example is your child seeing—bargain-
ing and manipulation, or open palms reaching out
in reliance upon Christ?

How could you and your child apply
the message of Psalm 34:17–18, and cry out
together with broken hearts for God's deliv-
erance? How could you cling together to the
"God-Who-Hears-and-Cares-Delivers-and-Saves"?

**Journey Marker #4: Moving from Depression
to Comfort in Christ—Our Comforting and
Encouraging Divine Counselor**

I cautioned Jared (and his parents) that as he
dealt with his fears, he might end up having to
deal more with his sadness. "It's like winning the
first round of a wrestling tourney, and then turn-
ing around and having to face the next guy who is
even tougher. Your fears may even be one way of not
having to fully face the fact that Grandpa is gone."

Now I leveraged my good relationship with Jared
to point him to the Better Counselor, the Best Counselor, the Divine Counselor. "Jared, it has meant a lot
to me that you've expressed how much I've helped
you. But I'm human. I can't always be there with you.
But there is One who will never leave or forsake you.
He will always be with you. He will always be *in* you!"

We then read together John 14 and the promise
that Jesus would send another Counselor to be *in* us

forever, never leaving us as orphans (John 14:15–18). I could tell how much it helped Jared to know that though Grandpa had left him, Jesus *never* would.

We then discussed what it meant to have the Spirit as our Counselor. "Jared, first this word *Counselor* means 'Comforter.'" I wrote on the whiteboard: *Co-Fortitude*. "The Spirit is in you to fortify you, to strengthen you. Jared, right when you feel those night terrors, how would it help you to picture the Spirit as your fort or fortress surrounding you and protecting you?"

After interacting about this, I wrote a second word on the white board: *En-Courage*. "Jared, the Spirit is also in you as your Encourager—to place God's courage in you. When you are facing those sleep anxieties and fears, how could you depend upon the Spirit as your En-Courager, giving you courage to face your fears?"

Of course, Jared wasn't dealing only with fears; he also was wrestling with sadness, loss, and grief. So I wrote a third word on the whiteboard—a word that might surprise you, because it seems way too theological. I wrote the word *Trinity*, and the words *Father, Son, Holy Spirit*. Then I asked, "Jared, would you like to see that you're not alone in your grief? Would it help to know that God the Father, God the Son, and God the Holy Spirit are all here with you to grieve with you, to comfort you, to encourage you, and to help you to hope in God?"

"Oh yeah!" Jared responded. So we talked together about the Trinity's comfort in these three passages:

Praise be to the God and Father of our Lord Jesus Christ, the Father of compassion and the God of all comfort, who comforts us in all our troubles, so that we can comfort those in any trouble with the comfort we ourselves receive from God. (2 Corinthians 1:3–4: God the Father's compassion and comfort)

Therefore, since we have a great high priest who has ascended into heaven, Jesus the Son of God, let us hold firmly to the faith we profess. For we do not have a high priest who is unable to empathize with our weaknesses, but we have one who has been tempted in every way, just as we are—yet he did not sin. Let us then approach God's throne of grace with confidence, so that we may receive mercy and find grace to help us in our time of need. (Hebrews 4:14–16: God the Son's empathy, mercy, and grace to help)

In the same way, the Spirit helps us in our weakness. We do not know what we ought to pray for, but the Spirit himself intercedes for us through wordless groans. (Romans 8:26: God the Spirit's groaning with us and praying for us)

Little by little, Jared found victory *in* his fears and hope *in* his sadness and loss. The fears did not magically disappear, but Jesus's presence gave Jared the courage to face his fears. Jared's sadness did not—and should not have—disappeared, but Jesus's comfort brought healing hope to Jared's tender heart.

Journeying with Your Child from Depression to Comfort in Christ

A counselor can be with your child one hour per week. You can be with your child many hours per week. God the Holy Spirit dwells *in* your child 24/7/52. As you comfort your child, how could you be pointing your son or daughter to the Divine Comforter of John 14:15–18?

How could you explore passages about the Trinity's comfort with your child, such as 2 Corinthians 1:3–4; Hebrews 4:14–16; and Romans 8:26? How could you apply Isaiah 53:3 and Jesus being a man of sorrows, acquainted with grief? How could you discuss passages about eternal, heavenly hope like Revelation 7:17 and 21:4 where there will be no more tears and sorrow?

Ministering Christ's Comfort and Hope to Your Child's Grieving Heart

By sitting in on our counseling sessions with Jared, Elyse, and Dexter, you've gained a glimpse into what could be going on in your own child's grieving heart—helping you understand and empathize with your child. You've also read a number of practical, relational, biblical principles for ministering to your child. In this final section, we want to expand on how to minister Christ's compassionate comfort and healing hope to your child's grieving heart.

Remember, children need good parenting even more than they need good counseling. You can be your child's best biblical counselor.

Parental Grief Ministry Principle #1:
Face *Your* Grief Face-to-Face with Christ

You've heard the illustration about what flight attendants say concerning a flight emergency: "Adults, first put on your oxygen mask, and then put your child's mask on them." Without your oxygen mask, you'll pass out and be of no help to your child.

Likewise, if you're not dealing with your own grief—in whatever losses you're experiencing—you'll be little help to your child. Recall 2 Corinthians 1:3–4: the God of all comfort, comforts you in all your troubles *so that* you can comfort those—like your child—in any trouble, with the overflow of the comfort you've received from God. The best comfort-givers are comfort-receivers from the God of all comfort.

Parental Grief Ministry Principle #2:
It's Normal to Feel Deep Emotion

Jared felt a variety of emotions: grief, sadness, fear, and anger. Death is an intruder, and grief has a piercing stinger that wounds deeply. Therefore:

Allow your grieving child to vent and lament. Don't force your son or daughter to "get it together."

Give your child permission to grieve. One of the most powerful ways to do this is by giving yourself permission to grieve and allowing your children to experience—to the degree they can handle it—your own sadness.

Mourn with your children when they mourn. Weep when they weep (Romans 12:15). Hurt with them when they hurt.

Practice lingering listening. Hear before you speak (Proverbs 18:13; James 1:19). Feel before you fix (1 Corinthians 12:26). Like the Holy Spirit, groan (Romans 8:26) before you guide (Romans 8:28).

Share your soul and Scripture. Our tendency is to rush in with answers, before we even hear the question, and before our child even knows we care about their concern. As parents, we can follow Paul's model of sharing Scripture and soul: "Just as a nursing mother cares for her children, so we cared for you. Because we loved you so much, we were delighted to share with you not only the gospel of God but our lives as well" (1 Thessalonians 2:7–8).

Realize that children's actions often express their emotions. Children rarely have the emotional intelligence or maturity to verbalize exactly what they feel. Their actions speak for their emotions. Seek to prayerfully discern what emotional message your child's behavior is sending.

Parental Grief Ministry Principle #3: It's Helpful to Prepare Where Possible

As you picked up in Jared's vignette, when his grandfather died, his parents could have better prepared him for what he was about to face. It's understandable that they did not—they were not prepared either. Nothing truly prepares us for death. But a couple actions and attitudes can help.

Pray before communicating. Elyse blurted out, "Get in the car, Jared. Your grandfather just passed away." Her communication could have been improved with a prayer, "Father, help me to share this difficult loss in the gentlest way possible."

Communicate before attending funeral services. Jared was ill-prepared for the incense, the chanting, and the open casket. Walk your children through what they are likely to experience. Talk openly with them about their questions, concerns, apprehensions, and fears. Also, seek to discern what your child is ready for. Depending on age or level of sensitivity, perhaps a child attends the visitation but not the funeral.

Parental Grief Ministry Principle #4: It's Possible to Hope

Not only give your child permission to grieve, but also *offer your child encouragement to cling to Christ.* Model for your child this clinging-courage as you take your grief to Christ your Victor, your big and loving Shepherd-King, your Deliverer and Savior, your comforting and encouraging Divine Counselor, who hears and cares. Model finding hope in the Trinity: in the Father of compassion; in the sympathizing, suffering, helping Son and High Priest; in the groaning Holy Spirit. Here are a few ways to do that:

Bathe your child in hope-giving Scripture. Grief, loss, casket experiences, and death can be the exact time when the Word comes most alive—what a paradox. The written Word points to Christ the Living Word, who is alive forevermore. Read Scripture together. Weep Scripture together. Cling to Scripture together. Pray Scripture together.

Relate God's story to your child's story. Picture it like this: You stand with your child between two worlds, between two stories—the earthly temporal story of death and the heavenly eternal story of life. With one foot, always pivot into your child's earthly story of grief, pain, hurt, loss, and confused feelings. With the other foot, always pivot together with your child into Christ's heavenly, hope-filled story.

Remind your child that you've read the end of the story. Life triumphs over death, hope triumphs over hurt, and Christ triumphs over the devil and evil.

> And I heard a loud voice from the throne saying, "Look! God's dwelling place is now among the people, and he will dwell with them. They will be his people, and God himself will be with them and be their God. 'He will wipe every tear from their eyes. There will be no more death' or mourning or crying or pain, for the old order of things has passed away." (Revelation 21:3–4)

We began with the greatest grief: death. We end with our greatest hope: eternal life. Christ conquers death. Christ empowers us to help our children to grieve with hope (1 Thessalonians 4:13).

Resources for Your Family Grief Journey

Baker, Amy, Editor. *Caring for the Souls of Children: A Biblical Counselor's Manual.* Greensboro, NC: New Growth Press, 2020.

Chandler, Lauren. *Goodbye to Goodbyes.* Charlotte, NC: The Good Book Company, 2019.

Fitzpatrick, Elyse, and Jessica Thompson. *Answering Your Kids' Toughest Questions: Helping Them Understand Loss, Sin, Tragedies, and Other Hard Topics.* Bloomington, MN: Bethany House, 2014.

Gibson, Jonathan. *The Moon Is Always Round.* Greensboro, NC: New Growth Press, 2019.

Guthrie, Nancy. *What Grieving People Wish You Knew About What Really Helps (and What Really Hurts).* Wheaton, IL: Crossway, 2016.

Kellemen, Bob. *God's Healing for Life's Losses: How to Find Hope When You're Hurting.* Winona Lake, IN: BMH Books, 2010.

Kellemen, Bob. *Grief: Walking with Jesus (Thirty-One-Day Devotional for Life).* Phillipsburg, NJ: P&R, 2018.

Tautges, Paul. *Comfort the Grieving: Ministering God's Grace in Times of Loss.* Grand Rapids, MI: Zondervan, 2015.

Tautges, Paul. *A Small Book for the Hurting Heart: Meditations on Loss, Grief, and Healing.* Greensboro, NC: New Growth Press, 2020.

Vroegop, Mark. *Dark Clouds, Deep Mercy: Discovering the Grace of Lament.* Wheaton, IL: Crossway, 2019.

Endnotes

1. Robert Kellemen, *God's Healing for Life's Losses: How to Find Hope When You're Hurting* (Winona Lake, IN: BMH Books, 2010). See also Bob Kellemen, *Grief: Walking with Jesus* (Phillipsburg, NJ: P&R, 2018).

2. *God's Healing for Life's Losses*, 10.